HENRY MOORE'S SHEEP

HENRY MOORE'S SHEEP
AND OTHER POEMS

Susan Glickman

SIGNAL EDITIONS IS AN IMPRINT OF VEHICULE PRESS MONTREAL CANADA

Thanks for continuing support to the Social Sciences and Humanities Research Council of Canada, to my friends, and, as ever, to Toan.

Thanks also to the literary journals in which some of these poems first appeared: *Arc, The Canadian Forum, Canadian Literature, Event, The Malahat Review, Matrix, Poetry Canada Review, Prism International, Rubicon, This Magazine.*
"Furniture Polish" appeared in *The Dry Wells of India*, edited by George Woodcock (Madeira Park, B.C.: Harbour Publishing, 1989); "Who's There?" and "Families" appeared in *Poetry by Canadian Women*, edited by Rosemary Sullivan (Toronto: Oxford University Press, 1989).
Some of these poems were also broadcast on the literary program "Fine Lines" of CFUV radio station, Victoria, British Columbia.

Published with the assistance of The Canada Council.
Series editor: Michael Harris
Cover design: JW Stewart
Photograph of the author: Toan Klein
Typeset in Monotype Centaur by ECW Type & Art, Oakville, Ontario
Printed by Les Editions Marquis Ltée

Canadian Cataloguing in Publication Data

Glickman, Susan, 1953-
 Henry Moore's sheep and other poems

ISBN 1-55065-004-1

I. Title.

PS8563.L49H46 1990 C811'.54 C90-090321-X
PR9199.3.G44H46 1990

Published by Véhicule Press, P.O.B. 125, Place du Parc Station, Montreal, Québec, Canada H2W 2M9
Distributed in Canada by University of Toronto Press and in the United States by University of Toronto Press and Bookslinger.

Printed in Canada

for my family

"The only living units that seem to have no sense of privacy at all are the nucleated cells that have been detached from the parent organism and isolated in a laboratory dish. Given the opportunity, under the right conditions, two cells from wildly different sources, a yeast cell, say, and a chicken erythrocyte will touch, fuse, and the two nuclei will then fuse as well, and the new hybrid cell will now divide into monstrous progeny. Naked cells, lacking self-respect, do not seem to have any sense of self."

— Lewis Thomas, "The Medusa and the Snail"

"These things are not secrets but mysteries."

— Seamus Heaney, quoting the sculptor
Oisin Kelly in "Glanmore Sonnets: 2"

Contents

I. HENRY MOORE'S SHEEP 9

II. DRIVING HOME

III. CAMERA OBSCURA 71

HENRY MOORE'S SHEEP
for Bronwen Wallace

NOTE

In 1972 Henry Moore dedicated his "Sheep Notebook" to his daughter. Published by Thames and Hudson (New York, 1980), it is a record of Moore's growing interest in, and affection for, the sheep grazing on his estate.

The first page of the notebook reads:

Subjects — insects

Tadpoles   *Sheep*

Birds

labyrinth

and whirring like moths   in lamblight

quick-wriggling in spring

melodious bleaters

amazing they are all

simply *Sheep!*

Page after page these
blunt-faced grazers, impassive as slippers;
heads wedges of darkness surrounded by barbed-wire.
Nature's doodles, scrawled with one hand
while the mind invents

heron

      apricot

           lotus

all things articulate and elegant.

Clownlike and tedious, their lumpen assertion
of mere presence.
As we expect.
As in "they're all a bunch of sheep."
As in the mob to which we most certainly do not
belong, being
if not elegant
at least strenuous pursuers of some moral or aesthetic imperative
unattributable to mutton at the mall
or at the polls
or to anything en masse except (perhaps)
hillsides spread with some purposeful flower
nature has provided to replenish our weary spirits
and to remind us that she deserves time off

after all

      for small amusements

           like sheep.

And then sheepishly, Henry
acknowledges their right to be,
to be there, in spring, dirty wet coats in the long green grass.

Insatiable.
   Mild.
     Happy.

Symbols of nothing but themselves —
their placid appetite an astonishment
to everything worried
or fierce.
And then he looks again.

And he sees the sheep have dark intelligent eyes; they regard him
without alarm but with a strange intensity.
He pencils this in.

Then he notices the long and lovely sweep of bone from forehead
to nose, and gives the skull
definition. The ears and tail emerge
from fleece, the tail an extra limb
more expressive than any penis, and he thinks
I have nothing like this
and suddenly envies the sheep.

It only takes a few pages.
And when he starts envying the sheep
they become female.
Those dormant blobs rouse themselves, heat rises from the page:
their bodies urge on the urgent suckling lambs
their tails beat time to the
pure unblushing springtime tra-la,
the hungers and loves
of sheep.

Sheep sheep

lambs/ sheep
sheep

sheep/lambs

sheep/lambs

Henry's notebook records
the holy families
of the fields.

And this is the strange part —
his sheep are more motherly
than his women.
They're all good sports in comfortable clothes
who never lose their tempers or
lament their figures.
They are playful and rueful and funny
and have the intelligence that comes
with love.

What is it about Moore's women?
Why do his women have less wit
than his sheep?

Great bleached pelvic sculptures.
Womb-hollowed matriarchs immobilized before
tall buildings, prone before the phallic etcetera towers of
modern commerce to whose gods they are spread
as sacrifice bare on the pavement.
Moore's women are the caryatids
of capitalist temples — every bank
needs one; every corporation can satisfy share-holder
and tax-man with a plaza full of Mama.

Earthbound, wide-hipped and heavy stomached,
balanced on haunches or elbows, propped on spindley arms,
with small heads and pinpoint eyes, thin-lipped smiles;
anacephalic, myopic, and gross.
Or bone ladies, ghosts of childbearing past.
Either way oppressed, and oppressive.
Either way, the body
as a terrible sadness.

If tragic, then heroic?
But still
body   body   body
organizing the space around it into
background, asserting presence
not relationship
past and future nullified in the moment's
insistence.

Even in the dyads
of mother and child there is this
isolation.
In the family groups each member looks
a different way;
each gaze pins a separate
vanishing point.

VII

How to account for this contrast?

The pastoral theme, perhaps, that old lie about *The Fall* —
Eve withdrawn into her sad mortality
and the curly ignorant sheep, O happy happy sheep
forever panting and forever young?

Or but a formal contingency, structural support
being required for sculpture — hence she's recumbent
in four dimensions while they frolic freely
in two?

Or what's Mo(o)re personal, implied
by the analogy, analogy by its nature
implying both likeness and difference.
As thus:
    the lambs are seen
    from the parent's perspective, the women
    from a child's point of view:
    Big Momma and little me.

So his tenderness goes to the sheep
and his ambivalence to
the human figures.

It figures.

VIII

Henry, not that you did wrong, but that you said so well
what we had heard for too long without hearing, the old rhymes:

womb/tomb

death/breath

bone/stone/moan

mother/other

and therefore made them finally redundant

And for the larger-than-life-size statement of filial guilt
confronting us in the theatre of public places
so that each action reveals its origin
in maternal suffering, its backdrop of maternal compliance
its fountain of mother's milk

For this we thank you

But Henry, there's more sentimentality in these
bronze heroines
than in all your fluffy lambs.

The middle of the notebook is full of sheep
and lambs and lambs and sheep
placidly eating in turbulent fields which
unravel into woods and the woods
into skies tied together with
wool, all one great ecstatic
snarl —

in the cosmology of sheep
everything's connected.

On the last pages of the notebook the sheep
are shorn.
Slack-bellied and heavy-uddered,
the poor, bare creatures
stand stark in that darkness
which defines them

but the oblivious lambs suck on.

DRIVING HOME

WHO'S THERE?

Where does the room go
when the lights go out?
The chairs, the blank wooden face
of the table close in
on themselves, into the secret life
of things which our life,
fitfully, interrupts.

I know this.
Crossed lines, especially
in spring; there is this
other life.
It's the same with the mountain, in snow or sun;
the same with the grey lake
by the grace of whose true creatures
I am permitted to explore.

See how carefully I swim?
Displacing very little water,
almost a fish, really;
quite recently a fish.

It is only parents who believe anyone
can be protected.
After all, that's their job.

Footsteps.
Now they are coming closer.
Now they are going away.

Hummingbird's flash and whirr over red
monarda, strange militant plant at odds
with its luring perfume. Hedged behind those soft spears
I watched, delighted. A bird as small as my hand!

Like dragonflies, those brilliant phantoms
with sapphire eyes, some creatures nearly
invisible, the more beautiful as they were difficult
to see. Once I found a star-nosed mole

stiff in death, improbable but delicate,
fallen on the path like a plucked flower.
Another time a tiny mouse drowned in a milk-bottle,
a grotesque warning against greed.

The earth teemed. Every flower cupped
an insect; even the water-lily — so chaste when viewed from
shore — revealed, close-up, its intimacy
with slugs.

Some things were ugly. Bats squealed down the sky
like tires on a wet road. We ducked them
as we ducked the bloated white bellies of fish
bobbing by us in the lake

or our mothers' voices calling us in to dinner
too soon, always too soon.
Grownups ate slowly, heavy in their chairs,
while the sap stirred so in us we could hardly

sit still. Out there, on the hill,
night fell. Acres of stars: another country.
I learned a few of their names but they grew
no nearer.

Oh I was a colossus in the world
of minnows, a minnow
as I swam through the trees.
So I learned the scale of things.

DRIVING HOME, I: BROTHERLY LOVE

It's the way the moon hovers over the trees and trails
balloon-like behind the car, that gets you —
not your brother and sister fighting for a window
or your parents' low-pitched gossip
wafting from the front with their smoke.
Some kinds of repetition give no pleasure: all this bickering
like the grate of broken bones, but the moon, the haunting moon
is something else.
Each time you turn to find it, your cold companion, with a thrill
of apprehension. Sometimes it's not there
(moonless night, night of winter clouds) sometimes
it startles you with its heavy copper stare
sometimes glances carelessly over a white shoulder as if *you*
are the one who is following.

Something you'll never understand.
One of the things.

The others don't seem to notice, or don't care, although you keep
pointing out the moon through the branches
the way someone with a stutter repeats the first syllable
of her name. The others wait politely for her to complete her
message; politely, but with discomfort and waning interest.
And so you stop trying to say whatever it is
and regard the moon surreptitiously, trying to outsmart it,
the way your little brother edges his head further and further
along your lap (you are the big one, the peacekeeper)
to bump into the head of your sister.
His black head, her blond one collide; tears, and rage;
smell of scalp
as you lean over to quiet them.

Later you'll put them to bed.
He gets a story, a new one each night, about magic.
She rejects consolation, writes instead
"Dear Diary, I hate my brother."
You try to tell her she doesn't really, but she knows
what she means — knows that he delights in tormenting her
and gets away with it because he's little
because he's a boy, and the favourite,
sneaking up behind her all the time, just there, waiting,
whenever she turns around.
Cold and unassailable as the moon.

SNOWFORT

We never suspected our feet till too late. They looked so capable, self-sufficient as seals in their black rubber boots. We were too busy anyway, in our beautiful fortress, to interrupt the building, the rising archways, palisades, architecture of delight; the visible, invisible white. What winters we had then! Fierce, and sunny; so cold the breath crystalized, embroidering the lungs with tiny needles, needles of ice. We had to watch each others' noses and ears for the blanch of frostbite. Not negligent, exactly, but distracted, stockpiling snowballs in our armories, refining secret tunnels, we forgot: suffered what seemed hours of agony afterwards, crooning *"It hurts, it hurts,"* over angry toes.

READING

It seemed I'd been waiting for this forever, when the letters danced together to make sounds, the sounds I heard in my head, or anyone's. When I first realized I was doing it I thought I was cheating, borrowing the "ook" from "book" to make "took" and "look," like copying someone else's tree in my drawing instead of making up my own: central pillar, three branches, a pillowy crown, five apples. Shouldn't each word have its own special, its own personal letters? But there could never be enough letters, enough angles and curves and loopy loops, to make all the words I knew and those I didn't know yet but would. And so I learned the economy of language, to borrow and copy and make do, remaking meaning. Someone else's tree in my drawing, curly smoke from the chimney, two windows, tulips all around. "Look" what I "took" from the "book"!

THE MAN NEXT DOOR

I.

When he touched me I knew it was my fault.
I thought about it all day and then I told
my Dad, I told my Dad so it wouldn't be
my fault.

He was nice, it was nice the way he touched me;
I was wearing my new bikini, I went
to show him. I felt grown-up. I thought he would
understand, he's the only grownup who really likes
to watch us. Maybe because he's lonely, because
he doesn't have a family or a dog or anything.
So I showed him my bikini.

The first one I ever had,
the first bathing suit *I* got to pick out, my mother let me.
Yellow and black, like a butterfly.
When I showed him he said "You look just like
a butterfly," and I was so happy, because he understood.

He's a nice man really, just sad because he has
no children. So he touched me. At first I thought it was a
mistake, he was reaching for his paper, over my lap.
Then he did it some more, kind of slow, like rubbing on calamine
lotion. It tickled. I said it tickled and he said do you like it little
butterfly and I thought he was trying to be nice so I
said yes. But then I got scared.

I don't know why I got scared, except he looked funny. His face
was different. I don't know. So I went home.

Later I told my Daddy. I know I did something wrong because he was a nice man, he used to watch us playing.
And then he moved away.

II.

It is a sort of vacancy, a mineral deficiency that leads a man
to eat dirt. In spite of himself. To spite himself;
to prove that the scornful tattoo he can feel on his pulse
is true: *Loser*, it proclaims *loser*, his own heart
running him down the way everybody did, even his Dad, saying
he'd never make anything of himself, it was in his blood.
So here he is now in a basement apartment at 50
listening to the family upstairs. Those kids running up and down
the hall — some days it drives him crazy, when he's watching
TV, when his team has a chance of winning. Other times
he likes to sit outside on the steps and watch them play,
little boys and girls, their plump unscarred legs
pumping away. The way the socks bunch up around their ankles.
The way their tongues hang out when they run.
Anyhow, they don't mind if he watches, they think he's OK —
that's the main thing. Sometimes they even ask him to
keep score, "Hey Mister" they say; he likes when they call him
"Mister." To them he is a grown-up just like
their fathers, he is someone who can drive a car.
What he'd really like though is to be "Sir."
He thinks about it sometimes, those white panties flashing
as they run, those legs, his father used to
beat him and he had to say Sir, Yes Sir, and his mother cried.
She cried when she was beaten too, she cried all the time, useless
woman. But these girls now — no one's ever laid a hand
on them, he knows, he lives downstairs, he hears everything.
Not that he wants to hurt them, he'd never really hurt them.
No. It's just those legs, so pink, teasing him from under
their uniforms; he'd like to stroke

those legs. He'd like to
undress them and see if they're soft
all over and he'd like
to stroke them a little, make them squirm, make them call him
Mister, Sir, Yessir, please do it some more. He knows
they'd like it, he sees the way they're always
touching themselves, and the girls, the way they
look at him, "Hi Mister," with big eyes,
flirting, all soft, they want it, they want it, one day
they're really going to get it.

DRIVING HOME, II: BREAKDOWN

There are people life grinds under its heel to such a fine powder
they grow ashamed of themselves and never recover.
Others call this "bad luck," as when
the rented car breaks down in a snowstorm, first day of
vacation, somewhere in the prairies,
or a minor plumbing job results in a flood through the ceiling.
For folks like this trains always run late
or tickets get lost;
new clothes are ripped or stained on the way to the party.
Initially the sequence of failures is just annoying
then it becomes funny
and finally, frightening.
Why me? cries the afflicted soul, sucking a hammered thumb,
picking up the shards of his glasses.
But he already knows the answer.
It's all because of something bad he did in fifth grade,
the hate thoughts he shot across the room at his rival
for team captain, who later got meningitis and died
in spite of the twentieth century.
Guilt, guilt.
You didn't do it, says his mother, offering a glass of milk.
But he doesn't believe her. He can hear the doubt in her voice;
the disgust when he first confesses and then the pause
as she considers her own unhappiness, her own manifold
failures. From his mother's example he already knows
this is a world without forgiveness.
And so he blunders into his future as into unblazed forest.
Just there, to his left, is a trail
leading to the picnic grounds.
It is littered with soda cans and gum-wrappers, all the detritus
of pleasure. Campers and dogs and children — so much noise

it's inconceivable he doesn't hear them, doesn't join
the long line of celebrants, those who expect good luck.
But he can't. All he can hear
is the whoosh of cars passing him on the icy highway,
the shatter and fall of glass.

CANOE LAKE: AN ELEGY

Cold still grey water in the lake where we plunged
at six a.m. to bathe; a salmon-coloured glow eastward
where the sky brightened. Shock of that water, its bite
of mountain ice against bare skin.
We were twelve or thirteen years old, shy
of exposure, giggling defiance, flashing
tough brown mosquito-bitten limbs and high white breasts
at passing canoeists. Strange men
in those days when all men were strange.

Trusting none of them but the guides who initiated us
into the mysteries of those woods. Woods we moved through
in moccasined silence, pretending to be Indians, shamed
by the smallest twig crackling underfoot.
We wanted to be absorbed into the scenery —
our red lumberjackets the first flags of autumn,
not warning signals to short-sighted hunters.
We wanted to be the people who aren't there
in a painting by Tom Thompson.

Being girls was so awkward. Not to pee
freely over the side of a boat but to squat stupidly
on shore. Not to be strong enough to portage a canoe
alone, or to carry the heaviest pack, the one
with the axe. To be so clumsy with the axe
that the guides laughed and rolled up their sleeves,
flaunting tanned muscles as they swung.
How we envied that power though we scorned their masculine
bulk and pelt of animal hair.

We competed for their praise, racing to put up the tents,
building fires from wood so green it smouldered
and went out or slender twigs
that consumed themselves at a spark.
Meanwhile the gods of our idolatry rolled cigarettes
and studied their maps. We preferred them
at a distance, like the great stags we glimpsed
lifting their ponderous dripping crowns
from the riverbed as we passed.

Nights 'round the campfire the guides told gruesome tales
of rape and murder, always enacted
exactly on the spot where we sat.
We loved them most then, their voices
blotting out the stars and the adrenalin of fear in us
indistinguishable from lust.
We thought we'd never sleep again, hugging ourselves
in the dark, vigilant for footsteps, inches from each other
but totally alone.
We fell asleep almost at once, perfectly happy.

BEAUTY

Maybe there are no easy deaths but Grandpa's
was terrible. The scuttling crab-wise crawl
of the disease eating him
for months, a slow insult.
The scotch-and-nicotine smell of him
gone off, festering,
so that even he flinched from his skin,
that strange dank leather
clammy as a wet groundsheet
stretched over his bones.
Bones he'd kept modestly hidden
in his patriarch's bulk, his executive jowls,
all naked and poor
in plain view — my fierce private grandfather
exposed.

My mother was afraid of him:
his *Sit up straight!* his *Girls
don't go to college.*
My sister, only little when he died, remembers
a scowling giant whose moustache spoiled
his kisses.
And he *was* fierce, his longshoreman's fists,
but with me he was always courtly. We discussed things.
And Grandpa, you were right,
which I knew even then, about beauty.
It comes from inside, you said (But I was only
twelve, desperate for power, afraid I might never
have any) *It has nothing to do
with fashion.*

We were sitting in your wood-panelled den, the TV on
to *Bonanza* or *Perry Mason*, your favourites,
and talking. And I knew you were right.
But even now I can feel that hard little knot, that "no,"
stuck in my throat like a candy
stolen from your secret cupboard and swallowed guiltily
and whole, that knot of stubbornness which, like the candy,
like everything I took from you, silver dollars, a complete set
of Dickens, your gold pen, was mine
from inside, my true inheritance.

SILVERPRINT

The leafless tree behind Great Aunt Edna's head is sharply etched as a master drawing but her face, shadowed by the broad-brimmed hat, is sweetly out of focus. She resembles Virginia Woolf, or rather Virginia Stephen; the same swan-necked langour, angularity of jaw, pouting lip. Not smiling, but poised.

My grandmother Dorothy stands in front and to the right of her graceful sister, sway-backed, grimacing into the sun. She's very young, a little chubby and clumsy. They are dressed alike in long buttonless jackets loosely belted over patterned blouses; both wear straw hats trimmed with flowers.

A small gingerbread house with a single chimney completes the picture; Edna leans on a fence. This is New York, 153rd Street, in April of 1919. This is before Dorothy married my grandfather and moved to Montreal and beautiful Edna followed. This is before Grandma taught me casino and gin rummy, took me to movies and let me try on her makeup; before egg creams on Edna's balcony watching heat-lightning over the city. I never saw this picture of them while they were still alive.

This is how I remember them now; two girls in springtime after the Great War. I dust the photograph in an apartment full of their belongings — Edna's table, Dorothy's chairs; Dorothy's pitcher, Edna's clock.

When Grandma was dying I came for a visit from England and she made me go back and died the next day. When Edna was dying I came on a visit from Toronto and she made me go back and died the same week. "Thank you for coming, darling" they both said, and turned away their silver heads.

KODACHROME

Except that Grandma never had silver hair, not in my lifetime. It was dyed red, and even after the chemotherapy she wore a red wig. This was her spiritual if not her natural colour; it went with the raucous laughter, the green eyeshadow, the charm bracelet whose golden trinkets I would lie in bed trying to remember: a tiny loving-cup, a ball studded with pearls, an amber seal engraved with an open pair of scissors.

Edna remained a lady and wore a blue rinse and pastel knit dresses. She made bran muffins and candied almonds and gave me embroidered handkerchiefs for my birthday. Not having children of her own, she took the role of Great Aunt seriously; she assumed the dignity of a grandparent with none of the attendant emotional confusion.

Once after Grandma died we were home for a holiday, my brothers and sister and I, being a family, filling up the house. For diversion after dinner we played some old tapes and suddenly her voice rang out loud and unexpected as a rock through the living-room window. There was more of her in that voice, more colour, than in any photograph. Nobody knew what to say.

Edna, though, remains a mystery; never more nor less here than in that captured image, April 1919, a shadowy beauty under a broad-brimmed hat. She was so passive and bewildered always; at the mercy of others' good wishes and capable hands. She cried when she knew she was dying because it wasn't fair and she didn't understand. But Grandma — Grandma took charge, shooed us away, pulled off her red wig and was ready to go.

DRIVING HOME, III: MEDITERRANEAN LIGHT

"People travel a long way to be able to say: 'This reminds me.' "
— Yehuda Amichai, "Songs of Zion the Beautiful, 29"

Bathing naked at Devil's Gorge with Carey,
dizzy on rhododendrons and sun. Letting the sun rove over
our bodies, younger then, resilient, brown and happy; happiest
like this, talking philosophy,
drinking the harsh resinous wine distilled
from pine trees and rain, drinking
a few sweet drafts of Greek, Homer or Seferis:

And if I talk to you in fables and parables
it's because it's more gentle for you that way . . .

Then — and this is not a parable, or if it is, not ours —
on the mountain-top we saw a flock of blue-
robed nuns
dancing with the children.
So we dedicated ourselves to the lucid gods
of the Aegean.

Over and over such scenes of dedication and renewal.
Over and over the lines at the travel agent, the lines
at customs. Paying duty; obeisance
to the wrong gods.
As though only distance from home and family
could permit us to hear our own thoughts.
As though distance itself *were* defiance, and our bodies,
transplanted,
could become something other than the shapes we wore with such
reluctant pleasure.

But irony's too easy, and not the point.
We both found and did not find something on that road which,
however circuitous back then, from this distance looks straight
as a highway.

The body dies the water clouds the soul
hesitates
and the wind forgets always forgets
but the flame doesn't change

we underlined emphatically in our books.
In fact, we still send each other postcards saying "Remember,"
trying to maintain what's lost in translation
from mediterranean light
although now we know that where we travelled was not a place
but a time
and that the deities who guided us might well have been found
back home.

THE LEAN-TO

Rain clatters on the roof, making you restless,
so you open the door. Cold air
and that acid green of spring leaves;
green of small snakes flicking red tongues,
snakes you know not to fear but pick up carefully
between thumb and forefinger
below the primitive brain.
Raw weather, and this urge of things
beginning; bud of horns on a lamb's head,
the thrust upwards painfully breaking skin.

Rain clatters on the roof so you go out on the porch
and watch the trees writhing;
there is no other word for it though they are not
like snakes. Their brains are not primitive
but classical and slow, a music of profound
intention. What happens here is pure reflex —
the wind plucks them and they throb —
but you like them best like this,
their strange abandon.

Rain clatters on the roof, it calls you so you go out
and lift your arms to the sky. No one is in the yard,
the dog's ball forgotten, and suddenly you are crying.
The rain is only a small thing: a child in a white nightgown
standing on the back porch with her doll
as you keep driving, 60 miles an hour,
down a highway with the radio on loud.
If you were about to cry already
it would get you going; otherwise not.
But you *are* crying.

Rain clatters on the roof, you go out into it,
into the trees and the wind, like you always do.
And the bark shines blackly; its ridges glint
like clams in the shallows of Lac Ouareau
where you played as a child, digging
for buried treasure. It shines like the stripped branches
of the lean-to you built in the pine woods
back of the house where nobody went
and a patch of bottle gentians lit up the moss
like a splinter of sky.
You always meant to take someone else there
but you never did.

Rain clatters on the roof and a few drops splash the window;
they slide down slowly and hang glistening from an invisible web.
The birds are lost somewhere in the tossing branches
calling each other home; the sky's getting darker.
When you played in the lean-to you were afraid to build
a fire. So many trees watching.
Some were ringed with white fungus like bracelets of bone,
others leaked resin you dipped twigs into
and set floating to watch the rainbows.
Once you tried to chew it, spruce gum;
you plucked grasses and sucked their sweet stems.

Rain clatters on the roof but fitfully now, an irregular
rhythm, the drummer half asleep.
A few birds swoop past the window, down to the earthworms
flushed from the soaking loam.
This is the best time to go fishing in Lac Ouareau;
when it's still raining gently at twilight the trout
rise to the bait, earthworms you buy by the pint
or dig up between the peas and carrots, the red monarda.
Mostly the trout are too small; mostly
you throw them back and keep on fishing, the sky
getting darker, nightjars slicing the air at the edge
of sight.

You keep on fishing and it gets darker; you hum a little
and flex your toes in your boots.
Tomorrow you'll go to the lean-to with something to eat,
you'll bring a novel and stay all day.
After the rain the ground will be damp, rotting leaves
over the pine silt, smelling of toads.
If you're lucky the blueberries will be ripe now,
you can live like an Indian.
If you're lucky no one will find you.

The mood of a day lived 10 years ago in a foreign country,
how it breathes in the bruised camomile, a few bars of that song
we never knew all the words to —

Distance softens everything; a soft lie.

His hands, Bob Dylan, the blue sweater,
cycling to Hay-on-Wye through a parting sea of sheep,
I love you in the parking lot:

beach glass. What didn't go down
with the ship.

Suspension in summer: blue lake under blue sky,
funky orchestra of frogs, the granddaddy buddha slaphappy
on the bass, yellow spatterdocks a
child's painting of the sun —

10 years still earlier, forever.

I once knew a man possessed of photographic memory.
Which is worse? 3-D and Dolby sound or this
selective sweetness?

What I wanted: life
in a Japanese room.
One branch of plumblossom, elegant hieroglyphic,
not all this old furniture.

The lure of minimalism is perfect control.
How a girl becomes anorexic.

But OK I surrender, only
let it be an interior by Matisse.
If full,
full of strong lines and sharp colours.

(1986)

LEARNING FROM FISH
for Lisa and William

They are tribal and territorial
and if you buy them in pairs they remain monogamous.
They dislike change, and are relatively incurious about
new neighbours.
Unless life gets too crowded
at which point somebody
gets eaten.

They are discrete in their depredations, leaving
no bones.

However this existential eugenics fails utterly to repress
the exuberance of the fancy-tailed guppy,
a small decorative creature whose prime motive seems to be
self-propagation.
One's tank soon resembles a sea of mobile feathers; this
may be pleasing at first if one takes credit for creating a
happy environment, a honeymoon suite for fish.
Do not do so, as the fancy-tailed guppy would spawn like crazy
in a mud-puddle.

Meanwhile the other fish are unhappy.
Alternatively sulking and snacking on the pied beauty
of the fry.
A monotonous diet.
Everyone is getting bored — all this spawning and eating and
spawning and yawning and snacking and sulking —

What is the meaning of life? ponders the Angel Fish,
meditative saint of these waters.

This is the point at which you give the guppies away
to Chinese restaurants with empty aquaria
or children with indulgent parents.
A further advantage to fostering out your fish is that
you can't blame yourself when they die
which they do with astounding regularity.

Sometimes they nurse each other until the end
as did dear Joey, a small spotted catfish
of Dickensian sentiment.
Joey of the warm heart and cold blood.
Joey of the furrowed brow and nervous, flickering fins.
A sort of piscine Florence Nightingale, he could barely eat
so faithful were his ministrations to his dying comrades.
He blanched when they sickened, recovering his markings only
when we bought him a mate.

There is something to be learned from fish.

They are utterly guileless
expressing affection or contempt with equal candour.
They live by appetite and are always hungry.
They are lazy, preferring tepid waters and modest dreams to
ambitious exertions.
They are not amused by plastic deep-sea divers
or treasure chests
littering the bottom of the tank.
They like real rocks, real plankton, real shrimp.

They never bite the hand that feeds them.

When you laugh it is all the unsynchronized clocks
in the watchmaker's shop
striking their dissident hours.
It is six blind kittens having the nipples plucked
from their mouths.
It is the ecstatic susurrus of prayer wheels.

When you laugh innumerable
pine trees shed their needles at once on one side
of the forest, indefinably altering the ecosystem.
A thousand miles away
two sharks lose their taste for blood,
mate, start a new species.

When you laugh your mouth
is the Mammoth Cave in Kentucky
and I can curl up there among the bats
intercepting their sonar.
Oh, your mouth is a diver's bell;
it takes me down untold fathoms.

And when you laugh, old dogs limp
to new patches of sunlight
which they bury for later, knowing something
about need.

FAMILIES

Once at the breakfast table when that harsh bitching
that passes for a stab but is really more like sawing away
with a rusty breadknife, leaving a jaggedy scar,
passed as usual in those days between my mother
and me my father began to cry
into his cornflakes. Big round tears for the lost family
on the cereal box; the one that was supposed to come
with the yellow breakfast-nook, the apple-tree
out back. Only one tree, our neighbour's, dropping its fruit
over the fence. Generous, but not big enough
to hide in, so there was nowhere to shelter, no option
but escape. But Dad had his job, his car, his sense of humour;
deep down hadn't he always known there *was*
nowhere else to go? That a family only keeps smiling
in photographs and even there
someone's always out of focus. Him, for example;
his eyes inevitably shut, as though caught by chance
between blinks, when really, it was a reflex, like sneezing.
He could smile or keep his eyes open — but not both.

I could make that a metaphor I guess, or quote Tolstoy in
Anna Karenina, but happiness in families is also complex
and not to be sneezed at. The problem is more with the way
we apprehend feelings in time. Sadness is so slow, a mule with
split hooves, picking its way over stone. Joy,
in this ratio, a 40's convertible, his first car,
speeding down green summer roads to a *doo-wap* refrain.
That is, when you're happy you don't have to know all the words,
humming along does just fine. But grief,
grief makes us all precisions, analyzing each other
to death: *You failed me, and this is exactly how.*

Meanwhile the evidence of our honourable if partial success
piles up — all those turkeys, ribbons, pots of flowers.
In their albums the smiles brave out our disregard,
bleaching a little with the years like the cedar dock down
at the lake, that worn path between the house
and the silent water: between what contains the family
and what it keeps them from. Lying on that dock with eyes closed
I told my mother all about you before we were married,
when I still wasn't sure; some of the old harshness in my voice
because I wanted or expected her to tell me not
to do it, to tell me the pains were more real
than the joy. But she didn't. No one could save me from my own
trip down that road; no one wanted to.
And so I jumped off the split grey boards into the reflections
of trees and clouds and swam away very fast from that house
to this one, into a new family. Eyes wide open,
but under water.

HEAVY WEATHER

I like this and fear it. The sky greyed for a storm;
that fierce brightness coming up behind clouds
like a slap on the face from someone you love, who loves you,
someone who did it on a dare and because otherwise
neither of you would ever have known the true appetite
of anger.

But what happens next?
Brightness falls from the air.
An interval of inconsequential thunder.
The leaves: fluttering hands of impotent bystanders.
And then an odd stillness in which the neighbour's skinny cat,
grey as a maverick cloud, stares at some enemy
no one else has yet acknowledged.

When the sky splits it is bright then dark then bright again
before the rain begins: a few drops, the merest fingertip pressure
to go on home. But it's not there anymore, home,
or you don't believe in it. What's real
is out here with all this terrible thunder
and the rain falling straight down now, so heavy
the trees stop tossing and stand quiet with bent heads
like pious martyrs, or with upright heads
like captive heroes in old movies about the Foreign Legion,
the ones whose hands never shake when they light their
last cigarettes.

It rains for a long time. Eventually you get bored
and go in, trying to remember what all the excitement
was about. And then it's just outside, the weather, and you're home
without knowing how you got there,
making popcorn, watching the late movie.
Just as you can never remember eating all that buttery stuff
so you can never remember the moment the wind came up
and the clouds gathered
and the first rumbles rolled in from behind the patient maples.
Now you just think lazily how good it is for the garden;
how fresh the air will be, after all that rain.

DRIVING HOME, IV: "IMMUNE TO GRAVITY"

First the fuss with baggage and tickets, announcements about
delays, overpriced coffee, then
slow manoeuvres
along the runway, building up speed, as we
mutter a little prayer or sit mute with bravado,
secretly examining the safety booklet which we already know
by heart.

Taking off we take off
sweaters and fuss with seatbelts, remark on the scenery:
houses shrunk to toys, the crackerjack cars aglitter
on the blacktop, and hey!
we're out of that traffic now,
how did we ever bear it?

And the bright shreds of conversation
flap flap on the line

peripheral but distracting until the lifting
gladness, earth pastoral green and brown, and then the
deep spaciousness of cloud the
cloud of unknowing who or where or what
we are only that we are
together held warm held high
you and I are home here
above the blessed planet.

A HOUSE
for Ioan

1. The Door

I love you so much that now I know
I have something to lose.
How terrible.
This is why love is denounced
from pulpits, crushed under jackboots, why men take their
poor tender bodies into the desert
to fast and howl at the sun.
It might be easier, they think, to be nothing
than to endure this kind of
dissolution. To be nothing —
a fieldstone, a wisp of straw,
a well where no light shines.
So they bury themselves upright.

But from the bottom of the well they look up
and see it: that bright
particular star. They will never
be free of it.
To love so much is terrible. Terror of losing
and of being lost; of having been found, found,
found out. Discovered so thoroughly that never again
can the world be simply open, a door
to anywhere, for now you belong.

The door is part of a house.
You open it, and enter your life.

2. Superfluous Fire

As though we were still small, hairy and cold.
As though this were forest, not city.
As though great and hungry creatures loomed in the shadows.
As though it were us or them.
As though we wore their furs through the long winters
and shivered and prayed to the god of the sun
and prayed not to offend the gods of snow.
As though I had borne you many children and they cried
and there was never enough to eat
and you went out hunting, leaving us alone for weeks
and I dreamed you were lost forever

we wanted fire in every corner of the house.
We just wanted it; two things we asked for
from our marriage house — fireplace
and garden, as though the hunting time, the forest,
the great cold were so imprinted in our cells that *shelter*
was another word for *fire*
and *home* for *land.*

The furnace keeps us warm, but it is a metal box
in the basement, a nagging voice, a machine
in a city of machines.
Give us fire to look at
Give us fire to pray to
For we are small and lonely and cold
and out there is the great forest.

3. Horses of the Night

O lente, lente, currite noctis equi!

I mouth   you eye   we skin
    as we turn to each other and turn
      to each other in the act
of translation

    My favourite line of Ovid not
slow enough, never slow enough to hold
    this moment   our pleasure

under the fine pressure
    of thighs the horses, massively black
      broad-backed and silent
run

4. crawl space

where there's only room for one I go
as you go
alone.

I hate you sometimes, sometimes
I need this dark:
leave me

alone
below this home we've made, a lie.
smell of bread baking

clean laundry on a chair
all simple, safe, and guaranteed
against apocalypse —

what nonsense!
(marriage a pillow we clutch
on nightmare nights)

look, sometimes nothing works —
no lullabye or myth —
aloneness is just

how it is, sweetheart.
so let me go down
under the house

that's what the space
is for.

5. Station Identification

All day doing little jobs around
the house, in and out of each other's
path — a sort of courtly
dance.

Carl Philipp Emanuel Bach's six
sonatas for flute and harpsichord playing
in the variegated tulips:
the conversation of minute but highly intelligent
creatures? or simply of yellow
and red?

Oh, kiss me you fool!

So this
is happiness. This
I like.

FURNITURE POLISH

Today my hands smell of labour —
garlic oil in the whorls of the fingertip,
oil of lemon in the grain of the wood.
Odours of mortality, of steady use, the ghostbody of action
like the sweet musk of your skin before your bath
or your faded flannel shirts
into which I press my face when you're away too long, husband.
Strange name I never thought to say in this life,
from the Old Norse by way of Anglo-Saxon, *husbonda*, freeman,
a person owning his own home and therefore in later usage
one who tills and cultivates the soil.
Later still, the correlative to wife, sexual partnership almost
an afterthought
or adjunct to the community of house and land.

Similarly with *huswyf*, a woman who manages a household,
especially one who does so thriftily and well — the property
took precedence. Logical, if unromantic,
at least to modern lovers, holding as we do that love
comes first and conquers all, even garlic
and sweat and unswept floors. The random dazzle
of the idea precedes the particulars
for us; thus the word *husband* became a possibility
on my tongue, and only then could I imagine the stubborn
dailiness of this alliance,
which one bends to eventually and caresses
as one caresses the known grain of an old family chair.
Things made lustrous with use earn this devotion
from us, inspire hope that, with time, we too
may deserve such love.

ONE

for my nephew Jonathan

"And when I found the door was shut
I tried to turn the handle but."
— Lewis Carroll

This is the year you will never remember.
You'll be told about it more often than you can bear; about how
you cried for 4 months, then sat up and grasped
the world. That you could *do* things — not just submit — changed
your disposition: you clutched and crawled
and laughed out loud. Became everyone's darling, who'd been
a holy terror. Oh, you taught us all respect, you
cunning cherub, first
of your generation.
But we'll get our revenge.
We'll tell stories about you, dotingly, over and over,
refining our memories. We'll anatomize you
attributing cheekbone and eyelash and nostril,
forehead and buttock and shoulder
to someone else. We'll distribute your talents impartially
among the needier of our relations
so they can share in your achievements.
We'll say *of course* to everything you do; as in
Of course he's a good athlete! Do you remember
those legs at birth? or
Of course he's moody; remember how he was
those first months?
And you, of course, will be excluded
since this is the year
you will never remember.

But what if you could?
What if you could reclaim for yourself, in yourself
what so deeply you awaken in us: this newness?
How the world is before the odd drift of things
congeals into familiarity; before faces, those pinkish blurs
of emotion, stiffen into fixed
identities —
before we assume we know anything at all.
And how it was for you when you started knowing;
we, the adults who pretend to understand you, assume
that was when you stopped crying.
But maybe that was when you started.

And yet again no, no dice, seeing your face so expectant,
so sure that today will be wonderful,
I know the rote skepticism of tired minds doesn't
belong here.
Sitting with you in the grass holding a flower,
the one flower in the world, all there is of yellow
in sunlight, so bright it startles you, you look at me and
seeing me smile, smile back your happy astonishment
that this thing can be here too, this flower you can actually
hold, and the dog who lets you pat her, her soft fur
almost the colour of the flower, you are overcome
and try to clap your hands
and who taught you that?
When I tell you the story will I add that you missed —
not having the co-ordination at 8 months to join palms on cue —
and that I wondered about the relationship of applause
to prayer,
something only you could tell me about, my angel.
But I don't suppose you will, because
this is the year you will never remember.

And then the next time I saw you, three months later,
you were walking — already, it seemed, reconciled to a
new point of view. Such nonchalance, such a swagger
of diapers! Little boy,
the dimensions you move through describe a
higher geometry,
any given point occupying limited space
but infinite time.
Which is why we want to stop you
if only in *our* memories.
You're about to touch down on that thick-aired planet we others
inhabit, where time is always too short
and the compass bewildering.
I just wish you a small reserve of the joy you have now
to go on with, that's all. The rest is best
as mystery, which is why

this is the year you will never remember.

(THE) OTHERS
for Rhea Tregebov

who we fear and grieve for, children
unloved or broken against the world's business
whose eyes accuse us, and not only their eyes
but ours
of pure dumb luck —

them, the others, whose wounds leave our children's skin
unscarred, whose hunger spares our bellies,
let us bless them

    for carrying away a little of the danger
    in their empty hands

    for being innumerable as the stars of heaven
    and as invisible in daylight

    for being statistics, the modern kabbalah
    in which we read our fate

and therefore let us bless our fear of them,
which is the last vestige of religious awe
as it was the first

    O spare us, Evil Eye

    Let the universe right itself and the meek
    inherit the earth
    but spare us too

Spare us to our proper work
and let us yet rejoice in righteousness
spare us to our children

or if not us
just spare our children

66

THE GIFT
(after a poem with the same name by C.K. Williams)

I never had it myself which is why
  I love kids so fiercely, seeing in them
the absolute purity of being in the present, absolutely
  in the present, with *tomorrow* and *yesterday*
or even *later* mere words, lying words, words adults use
  to deny you what you want right now — why shouldn't you
want it now? My hunger is real, realer than God or Africa,
  as every child knows.

Whereas I was watchful and anxious and trying to please
  and therefore not honest, therefore
a child adults liked but of whom other children
  were sometimes, not always, but painfully suspicious.
Once a girl at camp said she hated me and when I asked her why
  replied "Because you're always asking other people
if you can do things for them."
  I didn't understand her then but I do now.

As an adult it used to be important that children liked me
  because it proved that I was a gentle and spiritual
sort of being at a time in my life when all my ambitions
  seemed dirty; it was not much different from being licked
by stray dogs or tolerated by people's cats
  but I thought it a gift.
It consoled me for other kinds of loneliness, and seemed to purge
  my hungers of whatever might wound me too deeply

with mortality, but after all the children
   were never mine, so my flesh could resist their little
magnets of blood. In those days anyhow I mostly used
   other people's kids as a cover.
To escape the tedium of parties, of talking at parties,
   of eating and drinking in a roomful of people
all sadly looking for mates
   I'd be the one being silly on the floor with the kids.

I still enjoy being silly, on the floor or elsewhere,
   but now that I'm good at it
I don't necessarily have to involve people's children
   unless they too feel like being silly which they usually do
at parties. But what I see now as the gift is something
   different: their imperious appetites and abrupt
out-of-nowhere fatigue teach me the truth
   of the body, my body, middle-aged,

no longer so resilient, no longer reeling seven-minute-miles
   off an endless spool of track but instead, sometimes,
gratefully sagging into a cab with those bags full of groceries
   like someone on a sitcom I once might have sneered at
and thought devoid of proper self-respect, insufficiently serious
   about life. When my nephew gleefully pees in the pool
therefore I applaud. When my niece sings *Happy Birthday*
   for no special reason, I bake her a cake.

DRIVING HOME, V: GROCERIES

"But I'm not dumb; I know you only win when you bet real money
and play for keeps."
— Stephen Dobyns, "Kentucky Derby Day, Belfast, Maine."

So we load up the car (carton of eggs, tuna, tomatoes) like
all the other couples (detergent, tin-foil) and
go home (cans on the bottom, fruit on top).
So we drop off the dry-cleaning and empties,
a few old shirts for the Salvation Army,
pick up a newspaper, a pot of mums,
whatever.

This is any day now in this life
we, somehow, find ourselves in
without even trying
with small murmurs of protest and yearning glances at
black-leather lovers in cafés,
midwinter posters of Greek beaches,
whatever.

So we go out to dinner, bringing a bottle of wine,
and I wear makeup and you shave,
and the party breaks up at 10:30 because our friends have kids
and everyone's working, but we have a good time anyway; in fact
these days we find 10:30 is a good time to go home.
Especially in October when you can bite into the air
as into a tart apple
that same blend of perfume and ice.

This is what we like: to go for a drive into apple country,
sentimentality at full throttle. We like to
admire the leaves and throw them around and make great
dusty heaps of them; torn parchment, flaming histories of maple
and oak. We like to shuffle in them with our feet and then go
and buy groceries at a roadside stand
from an old woman in an apron
who makes her own pies.
We like to buy beans and squash and broccoli and apples
and some of her home-made chutney
and drive home with the groceries.

We like driving home with the groceries.
That's what home is, basically — the place you put
your groceries.
A trivial observation with far-reaching implications.
Including the groceries, including
the driving home.

CAMERA OBSCURA

MO TI; *fl.* 400 B.C.

Shadow hand plucks shadow flower:
both fade as the light's withdrawn.
Nothing lives without the sun, and shadows
don't live within themselves.

A man
has only one body
but sends many shadows forth —
as many as are the flames he stands before.
Thus a good man's influence carries far,
cast ahead by reverent minds.

So many mysteries!
A strong man walks carelessly, eyes fixed
on the road ahead.
He stops to drink rice wine, or shoot a bird.
The world bows down before him
whether he shouts or not.

Only in bedridden age
no one comes.
Now, when he would say *thank you*
if they did.

Thus in darkness we know light.

Shining forth,
objects send their images to us
like cries in a foreign tongue.

MUHAMMAD IBN AL-HASAN,
KNOWN AS "ALHAZEN": 965-1039

What it is is a dark room.
You can walk around in it.
When the world would dazzle you, when an eclipse
would hammer your eyes shut — see
how free you are, in here!

For your convenience
for your delectation
an aperture in the wall lets in a stream
of living light, projects
the sun's true likeness
on the opposite wall.
Regrettably, the image
is reversed,
but is this not an apt commentary
on the *modus operandi* out there?

A further curiosity
to be taken (if you will) metaphysically:

   the smaller the opening
   the clearer the image.

Our lesson: to keep to the straight and narrow
(the shortest distance between points) or,
more humanely,
to see things well
study but a little at a time.

Nothing. And nothing still. Then a sudden pulse: *fiat lux*. A point with no extension, a cosmic germ; the will-to-be clasped close to the source of all being. Lightning without thunder, the thunderclap yet to come. The love-cry yet to come. So time and space begin.

And begin again each time I open my eyes, engendering the world. You stand there in your body displacing air and I see through you; the gaze of thought redeems corporeal limits. That is, your body is a power acting on me; my perception of your image is potential knowledge. You send me love, love teaches me to see.

LEONARDO DA VINCI: 1452-1519

You may call it *oculis artificialis*
for it gives insight into sight.

How illumination comes from without
but must be received within.

How true and natural colours show themselves
only on a field of humble white.

Attend. Be faithful. The eye
frees us from the darkness of our cells.

Membrane, lens, machine, interpreter, god —
how everything makes sense, how worlds cohere.

They say Aristotle knew the principles, but friends,
I have mastered the practice.
My Academy of Secrets has revealed all things —
Nothing too slight or stubborn, nothing too awkward or quaint
for my inquiry.
Everyone stops too soon, I alone
have forged on.

On what —
mere speculation?
No, no, my doubting *amici*, on appetite!
I love this recalcitrant planet, its sneaky ways;
have faith that it will obey, indeed would prefer
Man's hand at the wheel.
Ergo, my *Magiae Naturalis* explains to you
just what to do
to elicit the powers awaiting your command.

The property of light stealing through a dark room
to relay its message onto any planar surface
was known to the Ancients.
But what did they *do* with this knowledge?
Shielded their fearful eyes from the eaten sun!
Left the image upside-down and gawked like brutes!
Note my refinements: long secret
but now revealed for your betterment.

A bi-convex lens in the aperture
will focus the image more clearly, transmit it thence
to a concave mirror which reverses
the Antipodes
projecting an upright picture on paper or screen.

The application? An Art which Nature makes and Man
can follow —
a perfect outline in light for the pencil
to trace!
Thus the goal of Art shall finally be fulfilled:
to imitate Creation with God's
own quill.

You see, my friends, how I work
for the common good —
with my invention,
each man can be an artist, each object
be tamed.
Imagine my pain then, to stand accused of witchcraft!
How can science be wicked? All follows
the Good.

Look.
These "deviltries" you condemn are simple
illusions. (If you feared yourselves less,
you would not fear such sights.)
The battles and castles and wandering knights
in mid-air
are a tapestry of light on a flickering screen.

Come, come, I'll explain.
Beyond this room I have built a sunlit stage.
There pimpled youths and minstrels play their roles;
there life goes on, as always, and in this room
as audience we watch, are moved, or dream.
To break the spell:
Disperse the beam
Tear down the screen
Open the door and see life as it is.

Are you not ashamed of your silly superstitions?
Do you not rejoice to have such noble
amusements?
For myself, I am full of wonder,
wonder and mirth.
Be glad, my friends;
use and enjoy all things.

JOHANN KEPLER: 1571-1630

".. . And yet, all the time I am playing I never forget that I am playing.
For we never prove anything with symbols: in the philosophy of nature
no hidden things can be revealed by geometrical symbols, but only things
already known can be put together."
> — 1608 letter to Joachim Tanckius,
> Professor of Anatomy at Leipzig.

Like Adam in his Eden
I give things names. But a name
is not a thing; the room remains dark
whether or not we say "darkness."

To get outside the box we must first know
we are in. Oh fruitful paradox!
Only difficult problems are worth
a life's attention.

My master Tycho had the keenest sight of anyone
but such obstinate ignorance.
And Galileo, that eccentric comet,
is too bitter and proud for a friend.

I choose the middle path — neither cautiously
clinging to preconceptions
nor running up-hill full-tilt,
heedless how stones fall below.

No lens can correct the vision
of these times. The medium of refraction,
our atmosphere, is
troubled and murky. But

the Heavens shine. They shine
and shine.
And in their crooked dance I see
our future.

ROBERT BOYLE: 1627-1691
(a select bibliography)

Some Motives and Incentives to the Love of God (1650)

The Usefulness of Experimental and Natural Philosophy (1663)

Experiments and Considerations Touching Colours (1664)

The Admirable Rarefaction of the Air (1671)

The Strange Subtilty, Great Efficacy, Determinate Nature of the Effluviums (1673)

Observations about the Saltiness of the Sea (1675)

The Style of the Holy Scriptures (1680)

Memoirs for a Natural History of the Human Blood (1684)

A Free Enquiry into the Vulgarly Receiv'd Notion of Nature (1685)

The Great Effects of Even Languid and Unheeded Motion (1690)

Of Seraphic Love (1693)

ISAAC NEWTON: 1642-1727

We live enrapt,
trying to correct the errors
of our eyes, but nothing
stands still — the very air
a perpetual tremor.

The star which I pursue
is a mirage, its light
lancing the skies at unimaginable speed
focused by a lens that bends its form
cast back into my eye, whose fumbling nerves
convey a broken image to my brain.

Why I look out: domestic life
breeds optical confusion
as in a dark room
things strewn before a sunbeam cast
swollen shadows.
What's close to us we can hardly see
at all.

Oh, the senses do their best but we must
do better. Although there's no white light
we can master the spectrum —
certain laws
invariable in a world of changing things.
And in this we find our peace.

DARK ROOM

I

Under all the fancy stuff
like a snake coiled around a corinthian column,
the primitive brain.
Here thinking stops, or is stripped bare
of its pretensions, a mere extravagance
of the cells.

The body sets its clock by available light,
releases joy or sorrow
as glandular secretions.
Bodies
mortal and celestial
govern our deepest rhythms.

Indignant, the cerebellum
strains after independence.
In its reticulated darkness
ideas race;
their connections spark.

If I say I choose to love you
what does that mean?
We also say *the right chemistry*
or ask *what does she see
in him?*

But we've known from the beginning, haven't we,
that light is a form of love,
all vision potential knowledge.
The city of glass and steel flares golden
at sunset
at the hour of going home.
And I always come home to you.

So the room is dark.
So we perceive only topsy-turvy images
of what's out there.
So we reconstruct the world in the obscurity
of our love.

II

What we remember: beauty
especially that for which
we did not ask.
Awed by the peripheral glory of things —
Weston's green peppers or the gossamer weave
of a shawl, mahogany sheen
of fallen chestnuts.

My friend's small daughter dawdles
down the street, entranced
by autumn leaves;
no two alike, each the most beautiful
until the next.
She wants to bring everything home.
She wants it all by her bed when we turn out
the light.

And like all children I played
at being blind — trying to smell colours,
to recognize a footfall, anticipate buildings
by a shift in the wind.
A riddling world I rarely enter, clumsy
as I am
my only compass my eyes.

III

Shining forth,
objects send their images to us
like cries in a foreign tongue.

But in dreams we're all translators;
eyes track enormous landscapes
where we've never been —
something in the cells
remembers invented history, something knows
what we need to see.

When I talk to you from sleep
and you reply
I am both here and there, in my dark room
alone and in
our marriage
as at the movies we hold hands.

Is it any different in daylight?
Would the answer give me *your* eyes?

Love, two worlds meet
and not lightly
when we embrace.

NOTES

The camera obscura is an optical instrument which, as its name suggests, originated as a literal "dark room" and developed into the photographic apparatus we call a "camera." This sequence traces the camera obscura's history from its origins in ancient China up to the time of Newton, recreating the voices of various scientists who worked with the device. Each poem developed out of reading about the life and theories of the figure named, and generally at least one phrase is taken from his work and is the germ from which the poem grew. The key phrases are:

Mo Ti: "Shining forth, objects send their images to us."

Alhazen: "The image is reversed."
"The smaller the opening, the clearer the image."

Bacon: "The gaze of thought"; and the idea that the world was created by light, as explored in his book *The Propagation of Species*.

Da Vinci: "Oculis artificialis"; and the observation that colours can be perceived accurately only on a white surface.

Della Porta: The events related in the monologue are historically accurate, though the words are invented.

Kepler: "The medium of refraction."

Boyle: All the titles are real books or pamphlets he wrote.

Newton: "In a dark room things strewn before a sunbeam cast swollen shadows"; and the ideas about the telescope and the spectrum.

SIGNAL EDITIONS

SELECTED POEMS *David Solway*
THE MULBERRY MEN *David Solway*
A SLOW LIGHT *Ross Leckie*
NIGHT LETTERS *Bill Furey*
COMPLICITY *Susan Glickman*
A NUN'S DIARY *Ann Diamond*
CAVALIER IN A ROUNDHEAD SCHOOL *Errol MacDonald*
VEILED COUNTRIES/LIVES *Marie-Claire Blais*
  Translated by Michael Harris
BLIND PAINTING *Robert Melançon*
  Translated by Philip Stratford
SMALL HORSES & INTIMATE BEASTS *Michel Garneau*
  Translated by Robert McGee
IN TRANSIT *Michael Harris*
THE FABULOUS DISGUISE OF OURSELVES *Jan Conn*
ASHBOURN *John Reibetanz*
THE POWER TO MOVE *Susan Glickman*
MAGELLAN'S CLOUDS *Robert Allen*
MODERN MARRIAGE *David Solway*
K. IN LOVE *Don Coles*
THE INVISIBLE MOON *Carla Hartsfield*
ALONG THE ROAD FROM EDEN *George Ellenbogen*
DUNINO *Stephen Scobie*
KINETIC MUSTACHE *Arthur Clark*
RUE STE. FAMILLE *Charlotte Hussey*
HENRY MOORE'S SHEEP *Susan Glickman*
SOUTH OF THE TUDO BEM CAFE *Jan Conn*
THE INVENTION OF HONEY *Ricardo Sternberg*

SIGNAL EDITIONS IS AN IMPRINT OF VEHICULE PRESS MONTREAL CANADA